The Future of Sports Training

Harnessing the Power of Virtual Reality

Table of Contents

Chapter 1. Introduction

In this exciting Special Report, we'll transport readers into the immersive world of sports training's future, where the lines between the physical and virtual worlds are continuing to blur. Welcome to "The Future of Sports Training: Harnessing the Power of Virtual Reality." As technology progresses at an unprecedented pace, traditional training methodologies are being redefined by the application of virtual reality. Making training regimens more robust, personalized, and immersive than ever before, this evolution holds immense promise. Whether you're a professional coach, an aspiring athlete, or simply a sports enthusiast intrigued by the extraordinary blend of technology and athleticism, this report is a doorway into the next era of sports training. Prepare to be inspired and enlightened by the game-changing potential that virtual reality brings to this arena - not just a technological shift but also, a reimagining of what's possible when you dare to go beyond the conventional. Buy the report today to get an exclusive look at this groundbreaking revolution!

Chapter 2. Setting the Scene: The Current State of Sports Training

In the world of sports training, the norm has long been a blend of physical drills, tactical strategy sessions, and mental conditioning exercises. While these approaches remain foundational, their isolated examination does not provide a complete portrait of the current state of sports training. One could go as far as to say that the era of 'conventional' training is giving way to a more innovative, technologically advanced landscape.

2.1. A Diverse Landscape

Sports training has always been multidisciplinary in nature. Just as in traditional education where math, science, social studies and more coalesce to form a holistic curriculum, the different aspects of sports training combine to create well-rounded athletes. Dietetics, exercise science, biomechanics, psychology – they exist in tandem within the training program, nowhere more evident than in elite sports training facilities around the world.

That said, while the goal remains the same, the methods have been steadily evolving. The integration of sports science has transformed training programs, often accentuating one aspect more through different periods of the athlete's development process or on their career stage. Some emphasize physical speed, strength, or agility, while others localize on mechanics or focus on mental resilience, depending on the individual's needs and sport-specific demands.

2.2. The Role of Technology

Technology has always played a vital role in sports training. Gym equipment, synthetic turfs, rubberized tracks, hydration and biomechanical studies, efficiency mapping - the list is extensive. For the average viewer, technology's presence might be most visible in equipping referees and umpires with digital aids or innovations that make spectator sports more engaging. For the trainer and athlete, however, technology is an integral part of the preparatory and development phases.

Biometric wearables, such as heart-rate monitors and GPS trackers, provide real-time insights into an athlete's performance, mapping a full spectrum of parameters from energy expenditure to recovery analysis. Video analysis tools help dissect technique, spot flaws or potential injury patterns, or study opponents' strategies. Advances in cloud computing and big data analysis have further revolutionized how these tools are used, allowing for greater precision in individualized training plans.

2.3. The Shifting Focus to Mental Conditioning

Historically, physical prowess was often the focus of training programs, and rightfully so. But as our understanding of sports psychology evolved, the tides are shifting. Mental preparation now shares the spotlight with physical conditioning, given the increasing recognition of mental strength as a vital determinant of athletic success. Guided meditations, neurofeedback training, resilience building workshops – these are all becoming commonplace in the training routines of elite athletes. Routines aren't merely schedules on a chart anymore, they are comprehensive programs addressing every aspect of an athlete.

2.4. The Emergence of Personalized Training

One poignant development in sports training has been personalization. Whether it's strength and conditioning, mental preparation, strategy development or injury prevention, programs cater to individual requirements. Unlike the homogenous 'one-size-fits-all' approach, modern systems leverage technological innovations to cater to the personal and particular. Using data-backed evidence and real-time monitoring, training is increasingly becoming tailored not only to sports or skill levels, but to individuals.

2.5. The Role of Virtual Reality: An Emerging Technology in Sports

In the context of technological progress, virtual reality (VR) represents the frontier. VR technology allows for an immersive and interactive experience, propelling athletes into a whole new dimension of training, with the promise of game-changing disruption. Although the technology is still in its early stages of adoption in this field, it holds great potential for developing physical skills, reviewing strategies, improving mental conditioning, and promoting injury rehabilitation.

VR's role in sports training can be compared to the introduction of high-definition video replay in tactical analysis. It is drastically different, yet capable of bringing a revolutionary change. As we teeter on the brink of this exciting advance, it's pertinent to examine how VR could reshape the entire landscape, altering not just how athletes train, but redefining what it means to be an athlete.

The current state of sports training is, in essence, a mixture of age-old philosophies and modern technologies culminating in well-rounded training programs. Riding the wave of these technology integrations, sports training is set to embark on a new journey – one that provides a blend of the real and the digital, to create training experiences that challenge, yet grow and evolve, the athlete. The era of virtual reality in sports training is just around the corner, poised to transcend barriers, and change our understanding of sports training and performance.

In the following chapters, we will delve into the finer details of these emerging technological advancements, particularly virtual reality, and investigate the changes they're set to bring into training routines. Brace yourself - the future of sports training, with VR at the helm, promises to be a thrilling ride.

Chapter 3. Birth of Virtual Reality: A Historical Overview

The virtual reality (VR) saga begins in the mid-20th century, long before the age of smartphones and the internet. However, to truly appreciate the magnitude of its influence on sports training, we must delve into its intriguing origins.

3.1. The Early Stages

Dr. Ivan Sutherland, often dubbed as the "father of computer graphics," pioneered the concept in the 1960s with the creation of the first head-mounted display (HMD), known as the "Sword of Damocles." It was an intimidating contraption due to its massive size but marked a significant stride towards immersive visual experiences. This primitive VR system, though rudimentary by today's standards, laid the groundwork for future innovations.

In the 1980s, immersive multimedia and virtual reality took a definite shape, albeit in theory, with towering personalities like Jaron Lanier introducing the term 'Virtual Reality.' This decade marked the birth of VR as we know it, with developments such as the Data Glove and the EyePhone Head Mounted Display. Although initially confined to the realms of science and technology, the foundation was gradually laid for its eventual foray into sports training.

The early '90s saw VR move into the public sphere, with Sega and Nintendo unveiling their VR gaming systems. Although these products were commercial flops due to technological limitations, they managed to bring VR into the common parlance, opening the door for future innovations.

3.2. The Advent of Modern VR

The shift into the 21st century was marked with more realistic, sophisticated applications of VR technology. While the initial Dreamcast and PS2 gaming systems didn't offer VR experiences, the release of the Oculus Rift development kit in 2012 rejuvenated the VR sector. Funded via Kickstarter, the Oculus showed the world that high-quality, immersive VR could be a reality.

This ushered a deluge of interest in the potential applications of VR, including its use in sports training. Teams and athletes from every sporting discipline began to delve into the possibilities offered by this now-accessible tech.

3.3. VR in Sports Training – The Early Encounters

The first applications of VR in sports training were rudimentary yet promising. During this period, simple algorithms and graphics were used to create virtual opponents or game situations for athletes to practice against or within. This allowed for specific skill training and a level of repetition that was previously impossible.

The NFL was one of the first major sports organizations to harness VR for training, with the Dallas Cowboys introducing the technology to enhance quarterback performances in 2015. This application allowed players to virtually experience game situations from any given perspective on the field. The technique was adopted by several other teams, attesting VR's potential for efficient, safe, and effective training sessions.

Simultaneously, virtual simulations started getting employed in sports like golf and tennis. They provided personalized, detailed, and instantaneous feedback that couldn't have been possible using traditional training methods.

3.4. The Rise and Enhancement

Despite the evident benefits, widespread adoption of VR in sports training was slow initially, due largely to the unfamiliarity and high cost of VR equipment. However, as technology continued to evolve and become more affordable, the integration of VR into comprehensive conditioning and training programs became more feasible.

The evolution of graphics, motion tracking, and processing power, along with the advent of products such as the HTC Vive and Oculus Quest, has vastly improved the realism of VR simulations. As a result, the technology's potential applications in sports training have broadened and deepened remarkably. Athletes are now capable of training in life-like virtual environments that can mimic the conditions of the actual game, helping them work on decision-making skills, strategic thinking and reaction times.

In sum, humble roots in the mid-20th century have grown into blossoming applications of VR technology, impacting diverse sectors and changing paradigms. The realm of sports training stands at a precipice, readying to dive into a more immersive, personalized, and efficient era of skill enhancement, thanks to the historical evolution of virtual reality. The chapters ahead will further explore the expansive potential and practical applications of VR in sports training. Prepare for a journey to the edge of reality as we know it.

Chapter 4. The Virtualization of Sports: A Technological Marvel

Sporting events have historically been associated with physically taxing exercises, showcasing brute strength, agility, and core athletic prowess. However, as we dive deeper into the 21st-century world of technology, a fascinating transformation is underway. This metamorphosis, driven by the onslaught of technological advancements, particularly in the field of virtual reality (VR), increasingly fuels the world of sports, training, and athletic performance.

4.1. The Rise of VR in Sports

The evolution of Virtual Reality (VR) has been nothing short of sensational. Initially setting foot into the gaming sector, VR has gradually but assertively made its presence felt in various sectors, with sports being a significant adopter. An increasing number of sports institutions, from soccer and basketball teams to professional Formula 1 outfits, are now harnessing the potential of VR to enhance the training and performance of their athletes.

VR does more than just replicate a real-world sporting environment. By leveraging cutting-edge sensors and programmed algorithms, it can provide real-time feedback, track athletic performance, and even anticipate future movements. This enhanced personalization facilitates the development of a more focused training regimen, fostering greater levels of athletic prowess. Moreover, VR can simulate high-pressure match situations, helping athletes develop emotional resilience and tactical acumen. Such immersive training is particularly beneficial in injury-prone areas, allowing athletes to preserve their physical health while maintaining a rigorous training routine.

4.2. Blurring the Lines: Physical and Virtual Worlds

The concept of VR in sports transcends the notion of physical space, even as it ensures the athlete remains at the heart of the experience. Boundaries between the physical and virtual worlds blur as VR provides a unique user experience, one that is controllable, replicable, and — perhaps most importantly — safe.

Remote training has suddenly become a viable and practical option, free from geographical constraints. Athletes can now access training infrastructures and world-class coaches from the comfort of their homes. Moreover, VR's ability to replicate any desired environment enhances the versatility of training sessions. Mountainous terrains, bustling city streets, or the quiet calmness of the countryside - all are just a switch away, catering to the varying needs of different athletic disciplines.

VR's unparalleled ability to generate data offers unique metrics and insight into athletes' overall performance. Detailed analysis of these metrics allows for personalization of training, tailored to the individual's skill-set, strengths, and areas for improvement. This ability is a clear demonstration of how VR has revolutionized the key aspects of sports training – emphasis, timing, and execution.

4.3. The Potential Challenges

As promising as VR seems, it's essential to understand that it is still a burgeoning technology with challenges to overcome. The financial cost of adopting VR technology might deter lower-funded sports outfits, not to mention the impact on traditional coaching methodologies. Many critics argue that VR lacks the "human element," thereby potentially hindering the development of integral aspects such as teamwork, leadership, and interpersonal relationships.

Moreover, there are practical challenges to consider, such as motion sickness associated with long-term VR use, or the risk of athletes becoming too reliant on simulated environments and losing touch with reality.

Yet, it's crucial to note that these challenges are not roadblocks, but rather stepping stones. With constant evolution and advancements in VR technology, such concerns are being alleviated. The magic lies in finding the perfect balance between virtual and physical aspects, thus maximizing the benefits while minimizing the detriments.

4.4. The Future of VR in Sports Training

As technological developments continue to rocket forward, the applications and functionality of VR in sports training seem nearly limitless. The future may well see VR being used for rehabilitation after injuries, developing game strategies, and mentally preparing athletes for high-pressure moments.

Highly realistic simulations, aided by machines learning and AI, could replicate competitors' tactics, allowing athletes to anticipate and strategize more efficiently. The VR training environment might soon be peppered with virtual fans to simulate crowd noises and pressures that come with competing in packed arenas.

It's an enticing prospect for sportspeople and technologists alike, as they strive to find newer ways of integrating the digital world into physical reality, enhancing the training landscape as we know it.

In this age of digitalization, the intersection of sports with technology forms an exciting nexus teeming with potential. The symbiosis of the physical and virtual worlds is a testament to our pursuit of excellence, pushing the boundaries of what's possible. As the silhouette of an athlete merges with the glow of the digital realm, we are witness to the birth of a new sports era: A world where athletic prowess, driven by the marvel of technology, has the potential to reach new heights.

This is only the tip of the iceberg. As we immerse ourselves deeper into the realm of VR, the training of the future promises to surprise and inspire us with endless possibilities. And while it marks a significant departure from the traditional, it's a journey that promises to be as exciting as it is revolutionary.

Chapter 5. Revolution or Evolution? Understanding VR in Sports Training

Tech-savvy sports enthusiasts and athletes alike have probably heard the buzz around virtual reality (VR) and its potential impact on the world of sports training. From creating immersive training environments to recreating specific game scenarios for practice, VR is promising to revolutionize the way athletes train and perform. But is it really a turn of the revolution's wheel, or is it an evolution? To fully embrace this innovation, it's indispensable to comprehend the depth of VR's involvement. Delving into the nuances of virtual reality, this exhaustive chapter aims to help you understand the phenomenon better, whether a revolution or an evolution.

5.1. The Birth of Virtual Reality in Sports Training

VR technology has been gradually infiltrating the domain of sports training over the past decade. Broadly, virtual reality creates an immersive, computer-generated environment which the user can interact with as if they were in it. First attempts towards integrating VR into athletic training involved stationary exercises with rudimentary headsets, a far cry from today's fully-immersive, spatial tracking models. However, these modest beginnings laid the foundation for an increasingly symbiotic relationship between athletic performance and technological capability, thus paving the way for evolution.

5.2. The Proliferation of VR Training

Contrary to the popular dystopian image of VR replacing the physical world, the genuine purpose of VR in sports training is to enhance, not to substitute. By creating immersive environments that can be altered based on specific requirements, VR allows athletes and coaches to individualize training. It also offers a degree of safety, allows more focused training, and helps in analyzing an athlete's performance in detail.

An athlete can don a VR headset and find themselves at a Wimbledon tennis court, pitchers mound at a full Yankee Stadium, or facing down a rugby 'maul' without ever leaving their training facility. The realism offered by VR provides unparalleled training opportunities without the physical and logistical challenges associated with real-world training.

5.3. Challenges and Potential Hurdles

But like any technology, VR in sports training too comes with its own set of challenges. High cost, technological requirements, somewhat unstable platforms, and limited content availability are among these challenges. For broader adoption, it is crucial for technology providers to address these hitches, making it more accessible and prevalent across various sports.

Moreover, acceptance and adaptation are also critical issues. Athletes, coaches, and trainers must be open to embracing the technological evolution and integrating it into their training regimen. As with any transformative advancement, initial resistance is natural, but educating and training users about the potential benefits is a necessary step for widespread adoption.

5.4. Implementations and Adaptations

Despite potential challenges, several sports have already begun harnessing the power of VR in their training routines. The American Football team, Dallas Cowboys, turned to VR to improve their quarterbacks' decision-making skills. By practicing in a virtual environment, the players can experience a full-scale, in-game scenario without any risk of injury.

Basketball teams are also using VR for skill training. It provides the athletes with an immersive experience of being on the court and assists in teaching and reinforcing fundamental basketball skills.

Furthermore, off-field, VR spells boon for sports psychology. It presents athletes with a controlled environment to practice mental conditioning. Research has proven that visualizing performance can be as beneficial as actual practice; VR takes it to a whole new level by providing an immersive visualization.

5.5. The Future Path of VR in Sports Training

The path forward for VR in sports training is brimming with potential. Thankfully, as technology advances and becomes more affordable, barriers to entry decrease. Continued research, dedicated solutions, and innovative applications of VR in training are expected to drive its uptake in the near future.

The integration of AI with VR could considerably expand the scope. It can assist in simulating more realistic opponents, track and review an athlete's performance in real-time, and provide feedback, thereby making the training session more productive.

5.6. Revolution or Evolution? The Final Verdict

Assessing the journey so far and future potential, the introduction and growing use of VR in sports training can be considered both revolution and evolution. It's an evolution because it harnesses existing paradigms of training methodology and takes them to the next level. However, given the majority adoption and expected radical changes, it also qualifies as a revolution, leading us to redefine how we perceive and engage with athletic training.

Emerging VR-based training tools and methodologies, and addressing challenges in implementation, will be the key to unlocking VR's full potential in sports training. With the promise of safer, more effective, and personalized training, the virtual realm is ready to redefine our understanding of 'real' in sports training.

Although the debate of revolution versus evolution may continue, one thing is clear; the future of sports training is brimming with immense possibilities, with VR at its helm.

Chapter 6. Case Studies: Success Stories of VR in Athletic Development

Football, baseball, basketball, and even lesser-known sports disciplines such as snorkeling and fishing are embracing the transformative power of virtual reality (VR). By integrating advanced VR tools into their training routines, athletes are empowering themselves with limitless environments and scenarios that help refine their skills, increase their spatial awareness, and boost their overall performance. We delve into different real-world applications of VR in sports training, spotlighting the success stories of professional athletes and teams.

6.1. American Football and STRIVR

STRIVR, a leading VR company in sports performance enhancement, has found significant uptake in American football, where split-second decisions are often essential to success. From NFL teams like the Dallas Cowboys and San Francisco 49ers, to college squads such as those from Standfrod and Clemson University, STRIVR's technology has achieved notable traction.

The VR program simulates in-game experiences, enabling players to immerse themselves in thousands of virtual play repetitions without the physical risks associated. The additional mental reps help players improve decision-making capabilities on the field and reduce response time. Dallas Cowboys's quarterback, Dak Prescott, attributes parts of his impressive performance to the numerous virtual repetitions facilitated by STRIVR.

6.2. Basketball with Intel's True VR

Basketball also uses VR technologies to considerable effect, with Intel's True VR being one such tool. The Golden State Warriors integrated True VR into their training program, helping players to engage in situational practice without physical exertion. Using a combination of high-definition video and sensors positioned around the court, the tool creates a 3D reconstruction of the court action.

It's a more intense focus on the game's spatial aspects, making players keenly aware of positioning, spacing, and timing. Stephen Curry, a record-shattering shooter, reportedly uses VR training tools for precise timing and shooting mechanics analysis.

6.3. Baseball and WIN Reality

Renowned tech startup WIN Reality is revolutionizing baseball training with their immersive VR technology. They've created a VR system allowing athletes to stand at the plate and experience pitches from specific pitchers. The pitch's speed, movement, and release point are all part of the simulation.

Several Major League Baseball teams, such as the Chicago White Sox and the Cincinnati Reds, have adopted this technology. The White Sox's first baseman, Jose Abreu, credits VR for his unique ability to anticipate and react to pitches efficiently.

6.4. Soccer and Beyond Sports

In soccer, Dutch company Beyond Sports is leading the way in VR training. Their platform uses game data to recreate specific match situations, allowing players to relive key moments and study opponents' tactics.

Ajax Amsterdam, one of the most forward-thinking soccer clubs globally, and several English Premier League teams, have integrated Beyond Sports' VR program into their training routine. They've noted considerable improvements in players' cognitive decision-making skills and understanding of game tactics.

6.5. Breakthroughs in Lesser-Known Sports

Moreover, VR is also carving a niche in lesser-known sports. For instance, Fishing League Worldwide (FLW) anglers use VR for experiencing different fishing environments. Divers also employ VR to simulate complicated underwater maneuvers and improve their technique.

As technology continues to mature, the applicability and utility of VR in sports training will only broaden. The blend of VR technologies with sports training methods heralds a future where physical ability, honed by hours spent in the actual field, blends seamlessly with cognitive sharpness, sharpened in the virtual world. An era where athletes perform on an edge, both physically and mentally, like never before. And a time when watching sports transforms into an immersive experience, blurring the boundaries between spectators and athletes.

Finally, it's crucial to remember that VR doesn't replace traditional training methods but complements them, offering athletes and coaches new and innovative ways to refine skills and tactics. The intersection of technology and sports is exciting and has historically led to remarkable breakthroughs. VR is the latest addition to that lineage: a transformative tool, redefining the future of sports training.

With whole new worlds of data accessibility, simulated real-world practice, accelerated learning, and tailored training modules, VR is a pioneering frontier. The upcoming years are set to witness its widespread adoption and refinement, effectively placing VR at the core of sports training and conditioning worldwide.

Chapter 7. Overcoming the Challenges: Addressing the Limitations and Risks of VR

As the application of Virtual Reality (VR) in sports training evolves, it becomes clear that mastering the technology presents its share of challenges. Determining how to effectively integrate VR into current training regimen still remains a significant concern. Here, we delve into these issues, presenting potential remedies and exploring ways of mitigating risk fundamentals to fully exploiting VR technology in the realm of sports training and development.

7.1. Understanding the Limitations

A fundamental challenge in exploiting VR technology in sports training is recognizing its limitations. The VR experience is a simulation, and while it comes close to real-world situations, it can never truly replicate all the variables found in a live sports environment. For instance, the tactile sensations in an actual game, the unpredictability of the natural environment, or the physical exertion involved cannot be precisely replicated.

Thus, over-reliance on VR can lead to players becoming too accustomed to the controlled environment it provides and may cause difficulty readjusting to real-world scenarios. An important aspect of handling this challenge is to strike a balanced integration of VR into the training program. VR should be seen as a supplementary training tool that enhances the training regimen and not as a replacement for traditional on-field training.

7.2. Technological Barriers

Despite rapid advancements, VR technology itself poses some challenges. The high costs associated with employing VR systems can prove prohibitive for many sports outfits, particularly at the grassroots level. Moreover, using VR requires a certain level of technical expertise. The need for continuous technical support and updates adds to the overall cost and operational complexity of the system.

To overcome these challenges, sports organizations can explore shared resource models or partnerships with technical universities or software development companies. They could leverage government initiatives or grants targeted at innovation and technology enhancement in sports.

7.3. Ensuring Athlete Safety

Another significant aspect of employing VR in sports training is athlete safety. VR is typically experienced using headsets, which create an isolated, immersive environment. However, prolonged use of VR headset can lead to symptoms like nausea, dizziness, disorientation, and, in some cases, psychological effects.

On the other hand, physical safety during VR training sessions is critical. The immersive VR environment can cause athletes to lose awareness of their actual physical space, leading to potential accidents.

Both physiological and physical safety concerns can be mitigated by setting clear guidelines for use and ensuring necessary precautions and supervision during the training sessions. Athletes should be encouraged to take appropriate breaks and maintain awareness of their real-world surroundings.

7.4. Evaluating the Performance Metrics

A pivotal challenge in the use of VR in sports training is the mismatch between the performance metrics recorded in a VR environment and the real-world scenario. It's essential that the metrics collected from VR simulations correlate strongly with actual performance.

A multi-disciplinary approach, involving sports psychologists, statisticians, and performance analysts, should be adopted to ensure that the VR metrics are representative of the on-field performance. Techniques such as machine learning could be employed to map and predict the athlete's on-field performance from VR-enabled training sessions.

7.5. Cybersecurity Concerns

Like any technology-driven application, VR bears the inherent challenge of cybersecurity. The amount of personal data collected by VR systems, particularly data related to performance, strategies, and health of the athletes, can make these systems prime targets for cyber-attacks.

In this context, it's critical that sports organizations and teams deploying VR as part of their training regimen have robust cybersecurity measures in place to protect data integrity and privacy. This includes secure data transfer protocols, firewall applications, periodic security audits, and integration of data breach detection tools.

In conclusion, the application of VR in sports training signals a promising future, fraught with potential. However, for the complete realization of its benefits, the understanding and addressing of the associated challenges are pivotal. Alleviating these challenges systematically and proactively will allow sports outfits to integrate

VR into their training regimens seamlessly, maximizing its potential while mitigating risks. The stakes promise to be game-changing. Sports training powered by VR is a compelling frontier, and those who dare to traverse it stand to gain considerably.

Chapter 8. The Player's Perspective: Athletes' Experiences with VR Training

Today's athletes live in an era where access to advanced technologies may play as much a role in their success as their inherent talent and rigorous training routines. Virtual Reality (VR), one of these futuristic technologies, has captured the interest of athletes worldwide, offering novel solutions to issues once thought insurmountable. Peer through their eyes as we delve into the profound impact VR training has on modern sports professionals, unveiling the benefits, challenges, and possibilities that lay in store.

8.1. Training Beyond Physical Limits

In the world of sports, physical strain is a constant companion. From countless training hours to intense game days, the pressure put on an athlete's body is extreme. However, VR brings forth an optimal solution by enabling comprehensive training sessions within the boundaries of a virtually designed space - a simulation known as 'presence.' In a VR environment, the risk of injury drops significantly, allowing athletes to practice their skills more precisely and push themselves beyond physical limitations without fear. Sprinters can perfect their starting techniques, golfers can refine their swings, and baseball players can practice pitch recognition, all within a controlled and safe VR setting. This extraordinary shift from traditional training provides athletes an alternative that effectively mitigates risk while maximizing the benefits.

8.2. Immersive Strategy Analysis

Historically, strategy analyses have been conducted through video recordings, chalk talks, and tactical board sessions. Enter VR, and the approach to strategic analysis is completely revolutionized. Players can now equip VR headsets to relive specific game scenarios from a first-person perspective, removing the constraints of two-dimensional screens. Defensive formations in football, basketball set-plays, or complex cricket strategies are now fully dissected, analyzed, and understood within immersive VR simulations. These virtual drills paint a holistic picture that successfully bridges the gap between theory and practice. Perhaps one of the most compelling features of VR is its ability to replicate the pressure situations faced during actual game play. The athletes, thus, not only analyze, but also, improvise in real time, honing their decision-making skills under stress.

8.3. Personalized Training Regimes

In sports, one size does not fit all. Traditional training methodologies often lack customization, averting some athletes from reaching their peak potential. Virtual Reality training, however, flips this paradigm. Using data tracking, VR creates personalized training programs tailored to meet the unique needs of each athlete and unlocks realms of untapped potential. In sports like football or basketball, the intensity of the training can pepper finer details like passing accuracy, shot selection, or movement execution. But VR effectively counteracts this by meticulously capturing the minutiae of each athlete's performance in the virtual environment. From analyzing the angle of a serve in tennis to the spin of a football during a free kick, each meticulous detail gets calculated, facilitating data-driven improvement in future sessions.

8.4. Real-time Feedback and Iterative Improvement

Traditional training methods are heavily reliant on a coach's experience to identify and rectify errors, occasionally making the feedback process exhaustive and time-consuming. VR training steps in to streamline this process by providing real-time feedback during each virtual training session. Integrated AI systems track the athletes' progress and instantly visualize their performance data, revealing even the smallest errors that might go unnoticed by the human eye. This real-time feedback motivates athletes to immediately rectify their mistakes and progressively improve their performance, facilitating an iterative cycle of constant refinement.

8.5. Challenges and Future Prospects

While VR training offers numerous benefits, it is not devoid of challenges. Some athletes report feelings of disorientation, nausea, or dizziness after prolonged periods in the VR world, symptoms categorized as 'cybersickness.' However, VR hardware and software designers are tackling these issues head-on, creating lighter, more comfortable gear and working to minimize motion sickness.

Moreover, the high cost of cutting-edge VR equipment poses accessibility issues for non-professional athletes or those based in regions with limited resources. On-going technological advances and potential economies of scale hint at future reductions in entry-level price points, which could democratize access to VR training tools for broader clientele.

As we forge ahead, the capabilities of VR in sports training can be expected to rise exponentially, highlighting the role of continued research and innovation. VR integration in sports is still in its infancy, awaiting full exploration. As athletes, researchers, and technologists rally behind this revolutionary technology, an intriguing future looms where the borders between the real and virtual worlds blur, further expanding the horizons of traditional sports training.

Finally, the players' perspective shines a light on VR training's ability to create an environment conducive to optimal growth and performance enhancement, transcending conventional training limitations. The question is no longer whether VR has a place in sports training, but rather, how this powerful technology will redefine the future of sports industry. Today, the athletes have spoken, and they cheer resoundingly in favor of Virtual Reality training.

Chapter 9. Future Projections: Where Could VR Take Sports Training?

Our investigation into the future of sports training anchored within Virtual Reality (VR) begins with an exploration of its potential trajectories, as the youthfulness of this technology belies its vast potential.

9.1. The Personalized Training Plan

Emerging VR solutions are centered around individual athletes' needs. Current methods heavily utilize generic training routines developed for various types of athletes. However, future VR sports training will allow input from a host of physiological and psychological factors, including age, sex, body composition, muscular power, endurance, athlete's mental state, and personality traits, to develop training routines tailored to individual needs. This allows athletes to maximize their potential, minimize their risk of injury, and optimize rehabilitation and recovery.

9.2. High Definition Immersion and Realistic Simulations

Existing VR technologies immerse users in a realistic 3D environment. Still, VR creators continue advancements towards making the virtual training environment even more life-like. Developers aim to enhance haptic feedback, tracking accuracy, 3D rendering, and display resolution, striving to deliver an experience indistinguishable from the real world. This kind of immersion should help fine-tune athletes' muscle memories, reflexes, and strategies in a replicated environment that accurately simulates real-world sporting conditions.

9.3. Integration with Biometrics

Biometric data is playing an increasingly prominent role in modern sports, offering deep insights into athletes' physical conditions. VR technology's integration with biometrics will allow these devices to monitor and track an athlete's vital signs such as heart rate, body temperature, and oxygen saturation level while operating within the virtual environment. Future biometric-and-VR integration will provide real-time feedback on athletes' physiological responses, enabling continuous adjustments to training intensity and approaches.

9.4. Interactive Multiplayer Training

Traditional training can often be an unexciting, lonesome endeavor. But with the rise of VR technology, we can expect a shift in this experience as training becomes social, immersive, and interactive. Athletes, despite being located miles apart, will be able to compete and collaborate in a shared virtual space, interacting with teammates or coaches, and even spectators.

9.5. Reimagining Rehabilitation

Rehabilitation is a critical aspect of sports training. However, it often gets sidelined due to its somewhat tedious nature. Through immersive game-based training scenarios, VR aims to make rehabilitation a more engaging and fun process. By employing motion tracking and soft tissue manipulation, VR technology can assist in the precise diagnosis and treatment of sports injuries, leading to personalized recovery paths and better results.

9.6. The Spectator Involvement

VR can also revolutionize the way spectators engage with sports. While existing VR applications give spectators the best seat in the house by placing them virtually courtside or in the front row of a stadium, futuristic VR sports training can potentially immerse audiences in an athlete's training routines. This would present a new lens through which fans can experience, appreciate, and respect the rigorous work that athletes devote themselves to, ultimately fostering a deeper connection and understanding between athletes and their supporters.

In conclusion, VR has tremendous potential to revolutionize sports training, making it more personalized, immersive, biometric-driven, interactive, rehab-focused, and inclusive for spectators. While we're in the early stages of this exciting transformation, the projections indicate an unprecedented wave of technological advancements that will drastically reshape sports training landscapes worldwide and redefine the athlete's journey towards peak performance. Empowered by VR, the future of sports training seems brighter, bolder, and packed with endless possibilities. The digital revolution is just beginning, and it's creating a world where the boundaries of sports training are continually expanding, moving us beyond the conventional and heralding the dawn of a new era in sports excellence.

Chapter 10. Societal Impact: Considering the Broader Implications of VR in Sports

The widespread adoption of Virtual Reality (VR) in sports training, while a technological marvel in its own right, holds profound implications for society as a whole. This revolutionary shift, as it culminates into mainstream acceptance, is anticipated to instigate changes in our understanding and practice of sports, with vast and far-reaching societal impacts.

10.1. Individual Implications

Firstly, the impacts on the individual level are extensive and varied. VR in sports training can revolutionize the personal development of athletes. With tech-enabled personalized training regimes, athletes can upskill at a pace peculiar to their abilities and learning style. A simple headset can transport them within an environment that is crafted to their unique needs and goals, without the constraints imposed by reality.

Moreover, VR can greatly empower athletes in remote or economically disadvantaged regions who may lack access to quality training facilities. This could democratize access to high calibre training, boosting diversity in sports, and opening unprecedented opportunities for raw talent worldwide.

10.2. The Virtual Spectator

For spectators, the fusion of sports and VR also signals a dramatic shift in how they can consume and participate in sports events. Think about viewing a football match not from your living room, but from the best seat in the stadium, without leaving your home. VR can fundamentally reshape the landscape of sports entertainment and fan engagement. This immersive experience has the power to create a more intimate connection between fans and athletes, effectively shrinking the global divide.

10.3. Ethics and Fairness

However, like any technological advancement, it's indispensable we consider the ethical implications. What does fair competition look like in a world where access to VR training tools could create a distinction between those who can afford the state-of-the-art technology and those who can't? We have an inherent responsibility to navigate these questions and instigate regulations to ensure equal opportunities for all athletes regardless of their economic background.

10.4. Health and Wellness

While the implications on physical health from VR training are largely positive, they urge a deeper exploration. Athletes are poised to benefit from injury prevention due to precise simulation of movements. However, VR's effects on mental health still need rigorous investigation. The blurred line between the real and virtual, while thrilling, could potentially lead to disorientation and distress if not facilitated with care.

10.5. Transforming the Business of Sports

In the commercial aspect, VR opens a new realm of possibilities for sports organizations and businesses. It promises to radically reshape the modes of revenue generation through unique fan experiences and sponsorship opportunities that this technology unfolds.

For instance, intricate data generated through VR can provide invaluable insights into fan behaviours, preferences, and engagement – intelligence that can be leveraged to offer heightened spectator experiences, enhance brand interactions, and ultimately, amplify profits.

10.6. Educational Perspectives

Finally, the educational sector stands to gain hugely from VR's foray into sports. Learners, whether budding athletes or students of sports science, can explore the intricacies of sports in a hyper-realistic, risk-free environment. This practical, hands-on approach to learning can facilitate a deeper understanding of the subject, thereby improving the pedagogy of sports education.

In conclusion, the societal implications of VR in sports training are profound and multi-layered. It holds the power to democratize sports, elevate the spectator's experience, challenge our ethical norms, enhance health and wellness, revolutionize commercial prospects, and accentuate educational experiences. As stakeholders – athletes, spectators, academics, businesses, and regulators – we are collectively stepping into a brave new world where we must fully comprehend and navigate these implications for better or for worse. With the anticipated benefits and potential concerns that come with this disruptive technology, the future of sports training is under evolution, written not just on the fields and courts, but also in the lines of code.

Chapter 11. Final Score: Concluding Remarks on the VR Revolution in Sports Training

In the pantheon of revolutions in sports training, the integration of virtual reality (VR) is gaining its mark, redefining what was once thought possible. As we wrap up this deep exploration of VR's significant influence and potential in sports training, it becomes apparent that this new technological frontier promises a bright, innovative future that carries the potential to revolutionize not only sports training applications but also athlete performance and spectator engagement.

11.1. The Athlete's Edge

When we examine the potential of VR in sports training, the target beneficiaries are undoubtedly the athletes. With advanced VR technology, trainers can tailor workouts and regimen to an athlete's unique needs and skills, driving both their physical abilities and tactical understanding of their sport to new heights. It's about transforming their perception of 'possible,' enabling them to make huge strides in performance through completely immersive training scenarios.

But the potential of VR in creating the ultimate competitive edge extends beyond training sessions. Using VR to simulate real competition scenarios helps in preparing athletes mentally, giving them a sense of what to expect in actual matches, but with the added benefit of practice runs without the risk of physical injury. No longer confined to their physical location or training facilities, athletes can explore diverse terrains, competitive situations, and challenging weather conditions, all from the safety of their VR environment. It's not hard to see why this innovative training strategy is quickly becoming a game-changer in sporting circles.

11.2. Personalized Training Regimens

One of the most transformative capabilities of VR is allowing customization at an unprecedented level. Sports are not one-size-fits-all, and VR has granted trainers the ability to mold programs to fit each athlete's unique physical characteristics and skill levels. The granularity of personalization extends to even tweaking the simulated opposition or game scenarios, testing an athlete's aptitude for decision-making, agility, and precision under varying points of pressure.

Inherent to the VR technology are capabilities to track and analyze data with high precision, further empowering customization. From the way an athlete moves, the accuracy of their shots, to their reaction time, VR can provide detailed data for analysis. Insights drawn from this analysis become instrumental in refining and adjusting training programs for continuous improvement - a concept previously unimaginable with traditional training methods.

11.3. Enhancing Spectator Engagement

While focusing predominantly on the impact of VR on athletes and training methods, it would be remiss not to acknowledge the potential VR holds for spectating sports. As immersive technology, VR transports fans from their living rooms directly into the pulsating heart of the action, offering them a first-person perspective of their favorite sports events. This newfound experience is redefining spectating, promising a future where viewers can virtually partake in the competition alongside their favorite athletes.

In conclusion, the VR revolution offers athletes, trainers, and fans a future that holds equal parts innovation and inspiration. It forces us to rethink what's possible, pushing boundaries in sports training and performance enhancement. It invites us to imagine an entirely new kind of spectating experience, where the line between player and observer blurs. It's a world in which physical limitations are lifted, opening up infinite opportunities for athletes to hone their skills.

While this new era of sports training is incredibly exciting, it's evident there are still challenges and uncertainties to overcome. The successful integration of VR into sports training will depend largely on ongoing research, testing, and the continued refinement of these technologies. As with any era-defining innovation, the journey will not be without its complications - but the potential rewards and influence are staggering.

By acknowledging VR as the most potent game-changer in sports training technology, we also accept the responsibilities and challenges that come with it. As pioneers standing on the brink of this frontier, it's our shared responsibility to ensure this powerful tool is used ethically, effectively, and for the benefit of the sports community at large. Virtual reality offers nothing short of an opportunity to radically reshape and enhance the world of sports training, and we are immensely fortunate to witness this revolution firsthand. Let's journey together to harness the immense power of VR, advancing the world of sports training beyond traditional boundaries - not just for the athletes of today but also for the generations of athletes yet to come.

Each innovative step we take in exploring, and leveraging this breakthrough technology contributes to paving the way to a new era - the age of Virtual Reality in sports. The future is brimming with potential, and it waits for us - not on some distant horizon - but right here, in the pulsating heart of the world of sports. Let's dare to turn the page, shall we?